A Keepsake

NEW HAMPSHIRE

Ken Paulsen

SCHIFFER
PUBLISHING

4880 Lower Valley Road · Atglen, PA 19310

Market Square, Portsmouth

INTRODUCTION

New Hampshire is one of the smaller states geographically, but it packs a lot of scenery, adventure, and experiences within its borders. From seacoast to the highest elevation in New England and all points in between, the Granite State offers endless trails to explore, Currier and Ives village scenes, old-fashioned train rides, plenty of water activities, and events that appeal to all ages.

Images on the following pages give a glimpse of the essence of New Hampshire.

It is no wonder that tourism is such a strong component of the state's economy—the season doesn't matter. When the "snow birds" travel south in the winter, they are replaced by the "ski bums" who long for the first snowflakes to fall. Hiking trails, which are generally open all year round, are busiest during the spring and summer. Fall provides its own unique color kaleidoscope that attracts sightseers from around the world.

If a personal visit is not in your near future, hopefully the next page can begin an armchair journey to experience the charm of New Hampshire.

Beede Falls, Sandwich

Gleason Falls, Hillsborough

Wild azalea

This sugar house in Antrim requires a constant supply of wood.

Courtesy of Eugene Willett and Dave Parker, Tap and Sap Sugar House

Hancock

Glencliff

Albany Covered Bridge

Not your typical sand castle

World-class sand sculptors compete each June at Hampton Beach.

Apple trees in blossom behind a barn in Hollis

High- and low-bush blueberries are a summer treat.

Wallis Sands Beach, Rye

Prentiss Covered Bridge, Langdon

Every llama deserves a morning walk through town.

Preserved barns, this one built in 1860, are a reminder of New Hampshire's heritage.

Bemis Brook Falls, Crawford Notch

Purple lilac is the official state flower.

Walter Harriman monument in Warner

Fire tower on Mt. Prospect, Lancaster

A view from Elephant Head at the top of Crawford Notch

The view near the top of Mt. Major

Abandoned bridge over the Pemigewasset River

Fields of lupine bloom from June into July

Great blue heron rookery, Monson historic site, Milford and Hollis

Independence Day parade in New Boston

Fireworks at Hampton Beach

Annual hot air balloon festival in Pittsfield

Winnipesaukee Scenic Railroad leaves the station at Weirs Beach.

Portsmouth

Summer isn't complete without concerts at gazebos like this one in New Boston.

Squam River Covered Bridge

Star Island (Isles of Shoals) buildings

Excursion boat docks in Wolfeboro

Star Island church

Crystal Cascade, Stark

Lower Ammonoosuc Falls

Cog Railway, Bretton Woods

Sanbornton

Jericho Mountain State Park, Berlin

Randolph

The Balsams, Dixville Notch

Beaver Brook Falls, Colebrook

Tamworth

Dixville Notch

Pemigewasset River, Franconia Notch State Park

Nelson

Kinsman Falls, Basin-Cascade Trail in Franconia Notch

Norway Pond, Hancock

Along Route 16 northeast of Errol

Hollis farm

Restored Ashland depot

Whitefield

Sentinel Pine footbridge, Flume Gorge

Gazebo on the Commons, Rindge

New Boston

First learn to stand up, then to ski.

Sled dog races are an annual event in Laconia.

Sap-gathering competition, Stonewall Farm, Keene

St. Matthews Chapel, Sugar Hill

Meredith

Corbin Covered Bridge, Newport

Cornish Flat

Wolfeboro

Dublin

Rural setting along Route 120 in Plainfield

Historic Shaker Village, Canterbury

Sleigh ride at Farm by the River, North Conway

The Ice Castle is a unique winter attraction in Lincoln.

North Conway

Freestyle skiers at Waterville Valley

A bob house village on Meredith Bay

Ken Paulsen was raised in the Midwest, where he worked most of his life in the information technology field prior to becoming a corporate instructor in South Carolina. He now resides in northern New England, where he has pursued his interest in photography, concentrating primarily on landscape scenes. His focus on the New England fall experience led to prior books *New Hampshire: An Autumn Sojourn*, *Vermont: An Autumn Perspective*, and *Vermont: A Focus on Fall*.

Cover design by Molly Shields

Type set in Bell MT
ISBN: 978-0-7643-5748-0
Printed in China

Published by Schiffer Publishing, Ltd.
4880 Lower Valley Road
Atglen, PA 19310
Phone: (610) 593-1777; Fax: (610) 593-2002
E-mail: Info@schifferbooks.com
Web: www.schifferbooks.com

For our complete selection of fine books on this and related subjects, please visit our website at www.schifferbooks.com. You may also write for a free catalog.

Schiffer Publishing's titles are available at special discounts for bulk purchases for sales promotions or premiums. Special editions, including personalized covers, corporate imprints, and excerpts, can be created in large quantities for special needs. For more information, contact the publisher.

We are always looking for people to write books on new and related subjects. If you have an idea for a book, please contact us at proposals@schifferbooks.com.